GIRAFFE
the silent giant

by Miriam Schlein ∽ illustrated by Betty Fraser

Four Winds Press ∽ New York

BY THE SAME AUTHOR

The Rabbit's World

What's Wrong With Being a Skunk?

LIBRARY OF CONGRESS CATALOGING IN PUBLICATION DATA

Schlein, Miriam.
Giraffe: the silent giant.

Bibliography: p.
Includes index.
SUMMARY: A description and history of the tallest
animal in the world.
1.   Giraffes—Juvenile literature.   [1.   Giraffes]
I.   Fraser, Betty.   II.   Title.
QL737.U56S34   599'.7357   76–7922
ISBN 0–590–07421–0

Published by Four Winds Press
A Division of Scholastic Magazines, Inc., New York, N.Y.
Text copyright © 1976 by Miriam Schlein
Illustrations copyright © 1976 by Betty Fraser
All rights reserved
Printed in the United States of America
Library of Congress Catalog Card Number: 76–7922

1   2   3   4   5   76   77   78   79   80

ONE

In the dark of night, in 1826, in a seaport in France, some men were leading a strange animal off a boat. It was not an easy job; the animal was about four meters tall—about 13 feet—and weighed almost a ton. In spite of her great size and weight and her strange shape, she was a gentle, timid animal. It was for this reason that the men were leading her off at night, when it was quiet, when most people were at home, and no curious crowd would form and possibly frighten her.

Can you tell from her shape what kind of animal she was?

She was a young giraffe—the first giraffe ever to set foot in France. Tied around her neck was a "saphie"—a strip of parchment with verses from the Koran written on it. This was to keep her safe on her long journey.

She was a gift the Pasha of Egypt had sent to Charles X, King of France. And she had arrived safely.

But once she got off the boat she refused to walk any further. Finally, a man on horseback, who just happened to be riding by, was able to get her to follow his horse.

What a strange procession they made—the man on horseback, the giraffe, the four Arabs who took care of her, followed by three cows who had been taken on the journey to supply the giraffe with milk.

It was a slow procession. Once again on land, after her long boat ride, the giraffe kept stopping to eat leaves from the top of each tree she passed.

This was in November. The giraffe lived in a stable in Marseilles through the winter. When the warmer weather came, they made the 650-kilometer trip (about 400 miles) to Paris, to the King.

All along the way, as they walked past vineyards, farms, and villages, the people gathered along the roadside to watch them go by. Can you imagine the excitement when they heard the giraffe was coming? Gendarmes from each town were alerted so they could control the crowds.

The people waited impatiently, for no one had ever seen a giraffe before. And they were even more excited when she finally came into view. They had never before seen or even imagined anything that remotely resembled a giraffe. They could hardly believe their eyes.

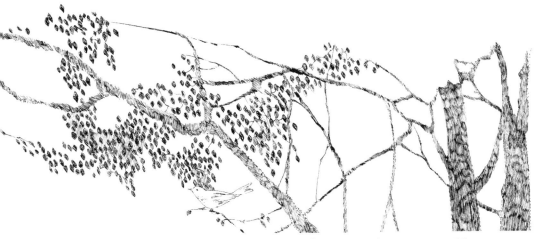

"Look!" they cried. "Her neck is as high as a tower!"

"The front legs are taller than the back legs."

"What a beautiful design on the skin!"

"It is a giant!"

"But not fierce. See how easily they lead her."

"She has gentle eyes."

"What a funny wispy bunch of hairs, dangling at the end of the tail."

"Such long legs. . . ."

"And how strangely she walks; see, first the two left legs go forward, then the two right legs."

ᔑ 5 ᔑ

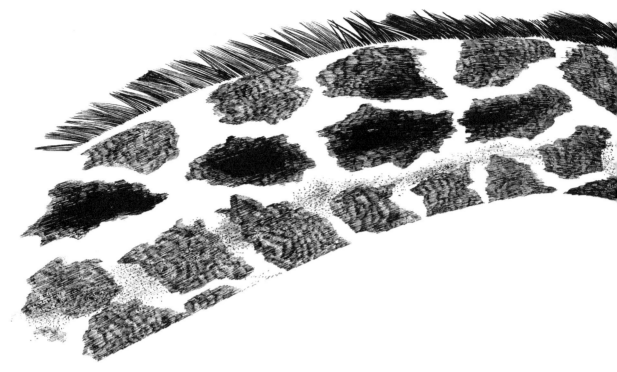

They laughed when she stopped and bent her great neck to lick
one of her Arab keepers with her tongue.

"Mon Dieu, look at that tongue; it is half a meter long."

They were agreed on one thing: this was a strange and marvel-
ous creature.

"If I had not seen it with my own eyes," said one old man, "I
would not believe it."

One early European artist drew a giraffe that looked something like this.

TWO

It is true—there is something almost unbelievable about the giraffe. The thing that is so startling about it, especially if you have never seen one before, is that the parts of it—the tall skinny legs, the solid body so high off the ground, the neck as high as a tower, and the slender head—just don't all seem to belong together on the same animal. And so people would always try to describe the giraffe and even name it in terms of other animals.

The ancient Persians called it a camel-bull-panther.

The Greeks called it a camelopard, because it had the shape of a camel and the varied coat of the leopard.

Samuel Johnson, in his famous dictionary, says the giraffe is "taller than the elephant, but not so thick."

An Italian traveler in Egypt in the 1400s, who had never before seen a giraffe, wrote this to a friend back in Italy:

> The Giraffe is almost like the ostrich, save that its chest has no feathers but has a very white fine wool, and a horse's tail . . . it has horse's feet and bird's legs . . . a long neck . . . and it has two horns.

In the 1200s, an Arabian writer described the giraffe like this:

Its head is shaped like that of a stag, its horns like that of cattle, its legs like those of a nine-year-old camel, its hoofs like those of cattle, its tail like that of a gazelle, its neck is very long, its hands are long and its feet are short.

Would you think all these people were talking about the same animal—or even that such an animal could exist?

Head like a stag

Horns like those of cattle

Legs like a nine-year-old camel

Hoofs like those of cattle

Tail like that of a gazelle

Long-necked

Very long ago, the Arabs believed the giraffe was so unusual that it did not even mate and produce young the way other animals did. They thought that first a male hyena must mate with a female camel. If the offspring of this cross was a male and he then mated with a wild cow, then a giraffe would be born.

In fact, everyone seemed to think of a giraffe as an animal that was sort of put together from parts of other animals.

But by the 1600s, scientists who studied animals began to feel that this sort of descriptive definition, usually colorful, vague, and often misleading, was not good enough. They began to sort the animals out and place them in different groups, relating them to one another on the basis of certain similar characteristics.

First, an English scientist named Walter Charleton felt that the giraffe or camelopard should be grouped with the camels. Later on, another scientist, an Englishman named John Ray, placed the giraffe in the genus (group) *Cervus*, along with the deer, the sheep, and the goats.

In 1735, a Swedish scientist, Carl Linnaeus, began a new and better system of "double-naming" the animals. Just as most people have a given first name and a family name, Linnaeus felt that animals would be better classified by two names: (1) a *generic* name, to tell the group the animal belonged to, and (2) a *species* name, to denote the particular, specific animal. Linnaeus kept the giraffe grouped with the deer, but called it more precisely *Cervus camelopardalis*.

But only 21 years later, in 1756, a French zoologist named Mathurin Brisson felt that the giraffe should be put in its own distinct genus, Giraffa, calling it *Giraffa camelopardalis*. This is the scientific name of the giraffe today.

At last the giraffe had its own identity. At last it was no longer treated as though it were a jumble of spare parts from other animals.

THREE

ZURAFA: *from the Ethiopic, meaning "slender"*
ZARAFA: *Arabic*
AZORAFA: *Old Spanish*
GIRAFFE

What is a giraffe? Giraffes are in the *Class* of animals called Mammals.

There exist about 4,000 different species of animals that are mammals—many of them quite different from one another. Bats, whales, dolphins, humans, elephants, mice, giraffes are all mammals. But the thing that all mammals have in common, and makes them different from other creatures—from birds, from reptiles, from fish—is that mammals are the only animals whose females produce milk with which they feed their young. The word *mammal* comes from the Latin word *mamma*, meaning breast.

An animal that is a mammal always (1) has a backbone, (2) has lungs and breathes air, and (3) is warm-blooded. This means its body temperature remains fairly constant and does not change according to the temperature of its surroundings.

There are so many different kinds of mammals that they are divided into 18 or more smaller groups called *orders*.

The giraffe is in the order called Artiodactyla. These are all the hoofed mammals that have an even number of toes (two or four) on each foot. Another name for this order is the "even-toed ungulates" from the Latin word *ungula*, meaning hoof or claw. Cattle, sheep, hippos, deer, camels, and giraffes are some of the even-toed ungulates.

*A very young giraffe whose knobs
are still under skin.*

But there are so many even-toed ungulates that these are divided into smaller groups called *families*.

Giraffes are in the "Giraffidae" family. Giraffidae are animals who have special kinds of horns that are skin-covered knobs that are present at birth.

There are only two kinds of animals now living in the Giraffidae family.

One is the giraffe.

The other is the okapi.

Each of these is placed in its own group, called a *genus*.   ✍15✍

Although these two animals are in the same family because of their skin-covered knoblike horns, still, they are quite different from one another.

The giraffe has a great tall neck; the okapi does not.

The giraffe lives out on the flat plains or savannah. The okapi is solid purplish color, almost black, with black and white stripes around its legs and buttocks.

Okapis live so deep in the central African rain forest that although they were known and killed by the Congo pygmies, they were not known as a special animal to the scientific world until 1901.

If there are significant differences between various types even within a genus, the animals in a genus can be further divided into different groups called *species*.

But all giraffes are basically very much alike. And so there is only one species of giraffe. This single species is broken into *sub-species*, which are types of giraffes living in different areas which differ only slightly in their coat color, their skin pattern, or have varying numbers of horns.

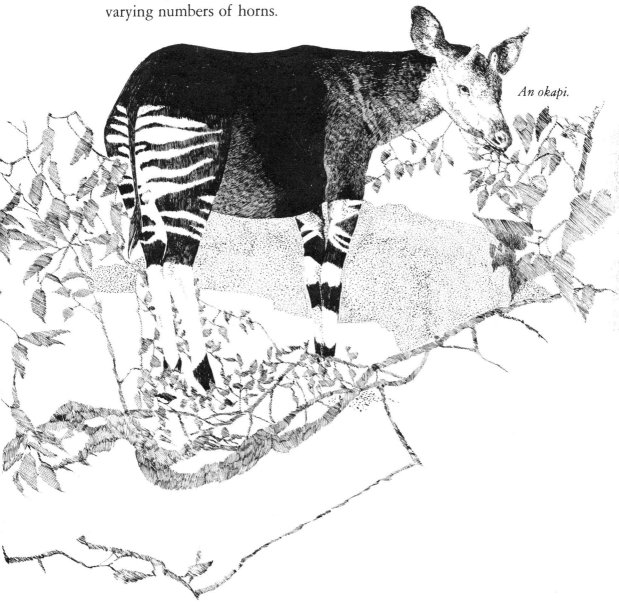

An okapi.

A palaeotragus from the Miocene Period. It was very similar to our present-day okapi.

FOUR

How long have there been giraffes? Long ago—so long ago that the earth's surface was not yet formed the way it is now—there were giraffids* roaming with other ancient mammals over what is now Europe and Asia. There were also giant pigs, saber-toothed tigers, and different sorts of elephants that had lower jaws shaped like big shovels with which they scooped up swamp plants.

This was in the time of the earth's history called the *Miocene*. This period began about 26 million years ago and lasted until about 5 million years ago. The earth's crust was still being twisted and shaped by geological movements. The Alpine and Himalaya Mountains were just being formed. The shapes of land and sea were changing, and not yet as they are now.

*Giraffids are members of the Giraffidae family.

How do we know there were giraffids living then? Because people have found giraffid remains, or "fossils" in the parts of the world that are now Greece, Spain, China, Israel, Persia, and many other places where giraffes don't live now.

They did not look like the giraffe as we know it now. They were different types. Some had short necks, some had long necks. Some had long twisty strange horns. They were lightly built and rather small. But they were the ancestors of the present-day giraffe.

About a million years ago, something happened that affected all animals. The Ice Age began. Before then, most of the earth was warm. Places that are now London and Alaska were tropical forests. Then, sheets of ice advanced down over most of the earth, driving all life before it. What were then warm, tropical parts of the world became arctic.

Many animals could not survive. They died off. They became extinct. Others managed to adapt to the new severe conditions. They developed thick shaggy coats and warming layers of fat beneath their hides.

The giraffe was one of the survivors. It no longer lived in Europe and Asia. It was too cold. But it moved on, along with many of the other animals, and survived in a warmer part of the world—in Africa—where it still lives now.

From about this time—for about the last million years—the giraffe has not changed. It has looked the same as it does today. The giraffe is sometimes called a "living fossil" because it is a species from the past that has continued to exist when other related species died out and became extinct.

How is it that some types of animals could survive and others could not?

The animals that survived were those who could change in some ways—in their shape, size, abilities—so that they could adapt to the new conditions.

How could they do this? How could they change?

Animals in each generation produce some young with slightly different characteristics. Some had more, some had less hair; some were bigger, some were smaller; the teeth, the hoofs might have varied slightly among animals of the same species.

What happened was that members of a species with characteristics that were helpful lived longer and had young. The helpful characteristics they had—the hair, the size, the slightly different hoof—was passed on to their young. Eventually, the basic species became modified so that all members of it had the characteristics that had helped certain members to survive in the past, and would help members to survive in the future.

That is how, for example, the horse as a species became larger and faster with a different kind of hoof and teeth than his ancestors had millions of years ago.

That is how the elephant changed even more so—from what was originally a small, pig-sized animal with no trunk to the way it is today.

This process of change is called "evolution." It is very gradual. It takes many many many generations for these changes to take place.

That is how the giraffe changed from a short-necked, slightly
built species to the way it looks now.

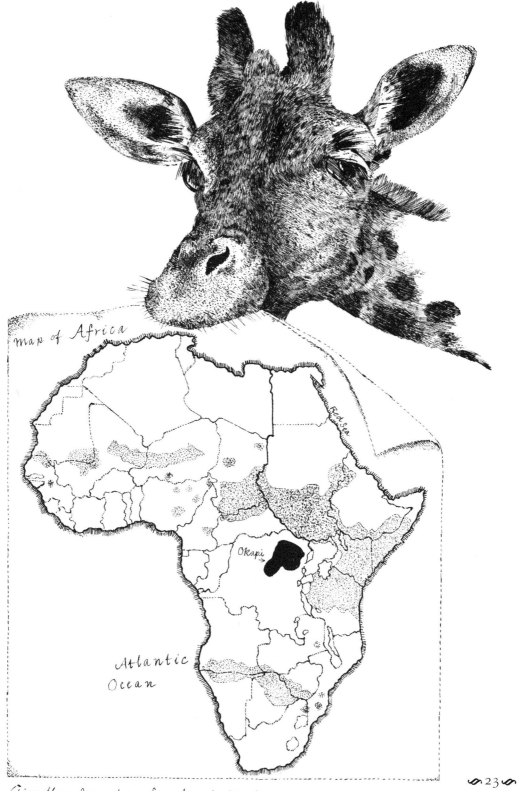

Map of Africa

Red Sea

Okapi

Atlantic
Ocean

Giraffes found in finely dotted areas

23

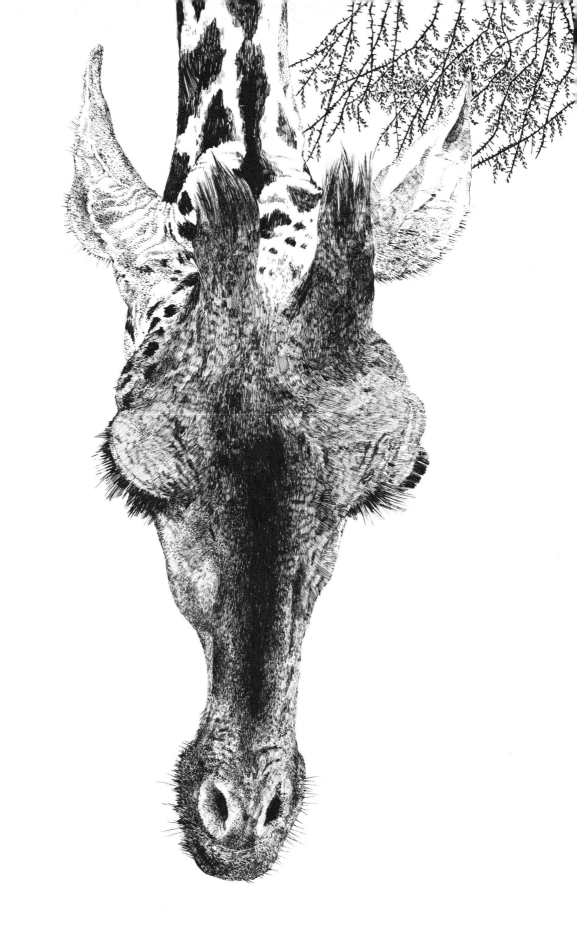

The present-day giraffe is designed for survival. The combination of characteristics that people find odd—all those parts that don't seem to go together—is just what has enabled it to survive. We can say that the giraffe is a triumph of evolution.

18 feet

9 feet

FIVE

Look at him.

He is tall.

He is the tallest animal in the world.

The male giraffe sometimes reaches about 5 ½ meters in height —or about 18 feet. The female is about 5 meters—or between 16 and 17 feet tall.

Can you think of the advantage in being so tall? That tall neck is like a watchtower. From way up there, giraffes have a good view of things. They have a good chance of spotting an enemy who is trying to sneak up. And so the giraffe's great height is an important thing that helps him to stay alive.

Female giraffes are generally more alert to danger than the males. Giraffes have two enemies—lions and man. If a giraffe sees one of these, she will give a snort of warning. Everyone runs. Their hind feet, moving together, swing ahead of the forefeet. The head and neck pump back and forth swinging around, almost making a figure 8. The tail is held curled over the back. They gallop as fast as 56 kilometers per hour—which is almost 35 miles per hour. Out on the flat, open savannah, a giraffe can easily outrun a lion.

And so giraffes' long swift legs are another thing that helps them to stay alive, and therefore has helped the giraffe as a species to survive.

But sometimes a mother giraffe with a young giraffe will not be able to get away in time. She will then have to stand her ground and fight. She pushes her young one to a good sheltered place—right in front of her body, between her fore legs. If the lion comes close, and tries to attack, the mother giraffe will strike out with a hard forehoof. A giraffe can crack open a lion's skull in this way. The giraffe, which often weighs between one and two tons, has power and strength.

Another thing that has helped giraffes to survive are their keen senses. Their senses of smell and hearing are very good. They have better eyesight than any other large mammal. And because of the placement of their eyes, it is possible for them to see in every direction without turning their heads.

When you first see a giraffe, probably the first thing you notice is his or her great height and unusual shape. But then you will start to look at the interesting pattern on its body. Some giraffes have a sort of cobweb design in white all over the brown body. Some giraffes have starshaped blobs of brown over a white background. On giraffes that live south of the equator, the design usually goes all the way down to the hoof. On giraffes that live north of the equator, the pattern usually does not go all the way down the legs.

This pattern on the hide of the giraffe is still another tool for survival. It is called "protective coloration."

Here is a clump of mimosa trees on the African plain. It is early morning. No animals are in sight.

But look more carefully. Do you see? There are legs standing among the trees. They are tall and thin and look like tree trunks.

Keep on looking. The sunlight on the mimosa blossoms makes a pattern of light and shadow. Almost hidden among the leaves are giraffes. They are hard to see. Their patterned bodies blend in 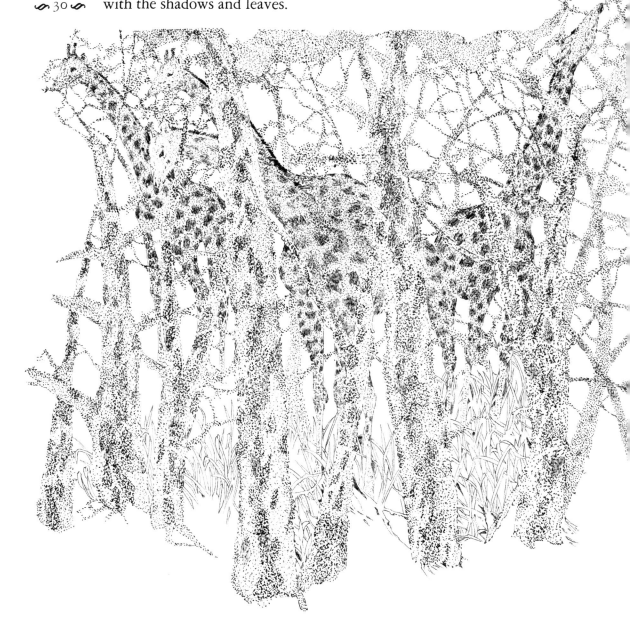 with the shadows and leaves.

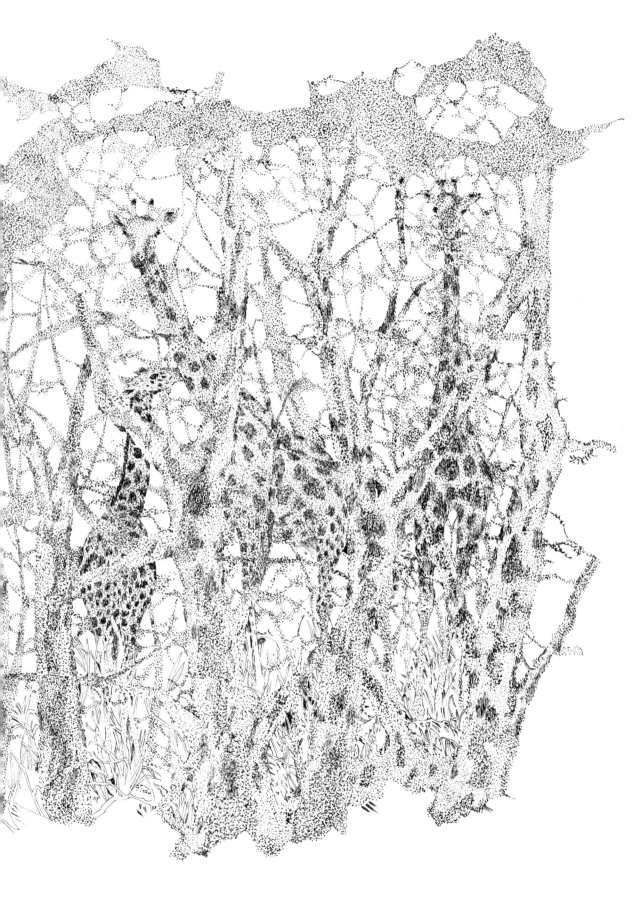

In the cool of early morning, while the dew is still on the leaves, the giraffes are eating. They eat quickly. The only things moving are their heads as they place their mouths around the leaves, then pull back their heads with a jerk, not biting but raking the leaves and pink and purple blossoms off the branches with their very mobile lips and their long muscular tongues.

The mimosa is prickly and has thorns. But the inner lip and tongue of the giraffe are covered with lots of pimplelike little bumps called *papillae*, and there is also a whole lot of saliva in the giraffe's mouth. These two things prevent his mouth and lips and tongue from getting scratched and hurt by the rough thorns.

They eat a lot, very fast, raking in the leaves and blossoms, gulping them down, then pulling in some more.

ᔊ 33 ᔊ

How do they eat so fast? They hardly seem to chew.

They can eat so much, so fast, because they have a special kind of stomach. They can let the food go right down without chewing it. Then, when they have a large amount of food quickly stored in their stomachs, they can go off to a safer spot. Here, they regurgitate their food, bringing it back up to the mouth. Now, when they have time, they chew it properly. This is called "ruminating." Animals with stomachs like this are called "ruminants." Now the food is swallowed again and digested.

Having a stomach like this is a big advantage to the giraffe. It's one more thing that has helped him to survive.

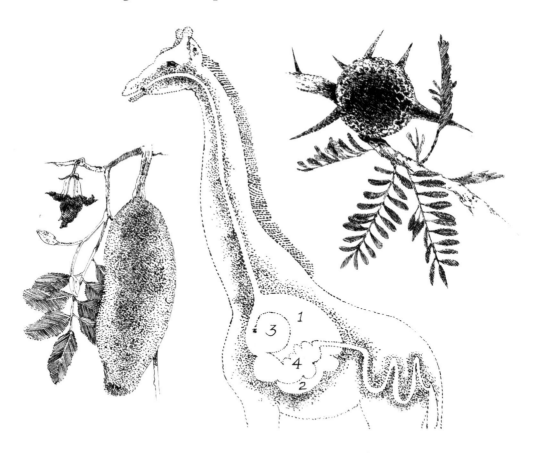

A giraffe has four parts to his stomach. One part stores the unchewed cud, and the other three parts digest the food after it is chewed. A giraffe belches, drools, and never has acid indigestion! Sausage trees and acacias are part of the giraffe's diet!

Six

Giraffes roam about searching for food and eating when it's cool, in early morning and evening. In the middle of the day, when it's hot, they rest. But they never all lie down or sleep at the same time. At least one member of the group will stand guard.

When a giraffe lies down to sleep, he twists his head and neck around, and rests them on his own back and flank.

Giraffes don't sleep very much lying down—only a few minutes. Most of their rest they get by dozing standing up, neck out-stretched, ears twitching, eyes half closed.

Does this position look relaxing? It is, for a giraffe.

When he is dozing like this, someone else is watching out for him aside from the other giraffes. It is the tickbird. This little bird lives on the giraffe. He takes sunbaths on the giraffe's back. He runs all over the giraffe, under his belly, around on his back, up and down his neck, looking for ticks, which he pulls out with his scissorlike beak and eats. If the tickbird sees danger, he cries out, then runs up the giraffe's neck to peck him on the head in warning. This partnership between the giraffe and the tickbird is helpful to both of them.

If there is water available—a waterhole or a stream—the giraffe will sometimes drink as much as 10 gallons at a time. But if for some reason there is no water, he can get by for weeks, or even more than a month without it. He can get by on the morning dew on what he eats, and on the water content in it.

A giraffe must be especially careful when he drinks. When he spreads his front legs and bends his neck to drink, he is in an awkward and vulnerable position. He cannot get moving fast if there is danger. So, before bending down to drink, he looks around very carefully. And while he is drinking, every once in a while he snaps back his head to quickly look this way and that.

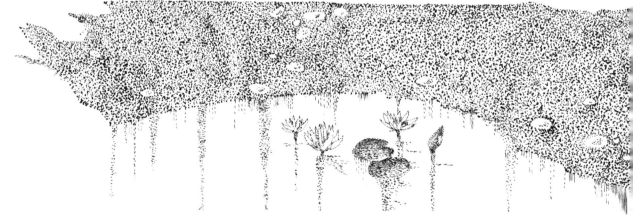

Another unprotected, vulnerable time for a female giraffe is when she is having a baby. At this time, she leaves the other giraffes and goes off by herself. It takes about an hour for the baby giraffe to be born. During this time, the mother giraffe is alone.

She is standing up. When the baby is born, it drops to the ground. But it doesn't get hurt. The mother giraffe nuzzles it and licks it clean. In about 20 minutes the baby can stand on its legs. And in an hour, it drinks milk from its mother.

A baby giraffe just born is almost two meters—or about six feet tall, and weighs between 45 and 68 kilograms, or between about 100 and 150 pounds. It drinks milk from its mother for eight or nine months, even though it begins to browse for leaves on lower branches when it is about three weeks old. It takes about four months until the baby giraffe can ruminate its food.

Only one giraffe baby is born at a time. Sometimes, in the wild, you may see several young giraffes staying close to one adult female. But this does not necessarily mean that the adult is the mother. Often, a female adult giraffe will watch over young ones who are not her own. It is like giraffe baby-sitting.

The baby giraffe grows quickly. At one year old, he or she is about three meters in height—more than nine feet tall. In six or seven years, he or she is a full-grown giraffe.

Generally about 10 or 15 giraffes will live and wander about together. There is a male leader, several females, some calves of different ages, and a few young males. Once in a while they will join up with other groups, and for a time will travel in a large group of 60 or 70. But soon they separate, and break up again into smaller groups.

41

Sometimes, male giraffes will fight one another. But they never use their hoofs against each other, as they would against a real enemy. They only use their heads, when they fight each other. They stand shoulder to shoulder, and push and circle around. Then one stands back, and swings his head against the other's neck or flanks. The other one spreads his forelegs wide to take the impact of the blow. Sometimes the blow is so strong, his forelegs are lifted off the ground.

When one of the giraffes has had enough of this, he gallops off. The winner runs after him in triumph, holding his head high. In these fights, giraffes never fight one another to the death.

Females do not fight in this head-swinging way. Their skulls are too delicate to be used as clubs. The male skull weighs about 11 kilograms—around 25 pounds. The skull of the female giraffe is about half this weight.

Most people think that the giraffe is completely mute. That is, physically unable to make any sound. This is not true. Giraffes have a larynx, or voice box. They just seldom use it. Sometimes, a giraffe will grunt or bleat. Once in a while, giraffes in zoos have been heard to make a gentle moo.

Mostly though, the giraffe is a silent giant.

Early travelers thought the giraffe looked like this.

SEVEN

"The admirablest and fairest beast that I ever saw was a jarref," said a merchant from London who was visiting Constantinople in the 1600s. And he was not the only person to hold this opinion. In fact, hundreds of years ago, the giraffe was considered to be a gift fit for a king.

In 1414 the King of Bengal received a giraffe as a gift from one of the African nations. The Chinese ambassadors at his court admired this giraffe so much that the King gave it to them as a gift to be sent to their Emperor. This is what one of the members of the Chinese court wrote:

> Amazing is this gentle animal, of strange shape and wonderful form . . . all are delighted with it. Wide open is the Reception Hall where the Emperor sits down to receive it. . . .

Later on in the 1400s the Sultan of Egypt sent a giraffe to Lorenzo de Medici, for his zoo at Fano. In April of 1489, Anne de Beaujeu, the daughter of King Louis XI of France, wrote to Lorenzo:

> You know that . . . you advised me . . . that you would send me the Giraffe. . . . I beg you to deliver the animal to me . . . for this is the beast of the world that I have the greatest desire to see.

She must have been disappointed, because Lorenzo never sent her the giraffe.

The people of the Kamasia tribe in Kenya called their god Mba. And they thought of him as looking like a giraffe with no horns.

However, among most other Africans, the giraffe was considered just a creature to be hunted for practical purposes. They trapped them in pits and snares, and killed them. They ate the giraffe meat, which was tough but had a good flavor. They used the thick hide to cover shields, and to make reins and whips. The sinews they used for making strings of musical instruments. And they used the tough hair of the tail as thread for sewing, or for stringing beads, or to make fly whisks.

It is sad to think of an animal like a giraffe being killed to make fly whisks and string for beads. But it is sadder still to think of the giraffe being killed just for what is called "sport."

This is what one English hunter in the 1800s wrote about a giraffe that he killed:

> Mute, dignified and majestic stood the unfortunate victim, occasionally stooping his elastic neck toward his persecutor, the tears trickling from the lashes of his dark humid eyes, as broadside after broadside was poured into his brawny front.
>
> His drooping head sinks gradually low, and thro' his side, the last drops ebbing slow from the red gash, fall heavy, one by one. . . .
>
> Presently a convulsive shivering seized his limbs—his coat stood on end—his lofty form began to totter—and at the seventeenth discharge from the deadly grooved bore, like a falling minaret, bowing his graceful head from the skies, his proud form was prostrate in the dust.

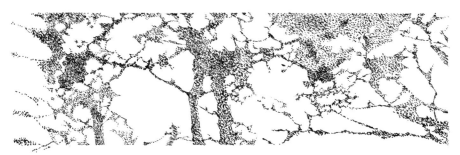

Can you imagine getting pleasure out of killing a big beautiful creature who is turning and looking at you with tears coming out of his eyes? Why not just admire him, and let him live?

In some countries, giraffes may be killed if there are a great many of them and they are destroying vegetation. In many other countries, giraffes are now a protected species. It is illegal to hunt them and kill them for sport. This protection is fortunate for the giraffes, and it is fortunate for us as well. Because the giraffe is a beautiful, unique creature, with a dignity of life all its own. It would be a loss for all of us if they some day were all to be killed, and no more of them were to exist in the world.

EIGHT

Now, it is no longer just the pleasure of Emperors and Kings and Princesses to be able to see and admire a giraffe. In most countries there are public zoos, where all of us have the chance to see a giraffe. In 1874, the first giraffes were brought to the United States. One female and five males were bought from animal dealers, and taken to the Philadelphia Zoo. There are now many different zoos in this country where you can see a giraffe.

At the time this book was written, there were six giraffes in the New York Zoological Park (The Bronx Zoo). Two were mothers with their two young ones. One of the young was a year old; the other was a year and four months. Their bodies were honey-brown with a white webbed design which went down to their knees. Below the knee, their legs were plain tan. Running along the top of their necks they had a short brown tufted mane about five centimeters high—almost two inches. They were in an outdoor cage, and walked about constantly. At the end of their tails were dark tail hairs 30 centimeters (about one foot) long, almost black. One of the young ones had no hairs at the end of his tail. I asked the keeper about this. He told me they had been accidentally pulled out when the two young ones were playing.

Inside, in different cages, were two larger, older giraffes—one male, one female. I watched while the keeper put some chopped apples and carrots and grain into their feed boxes, which were fastened high up on the bars so they could reach them easily. Then he gave them some bananas, which they sucked in whole with their strong lips and tongues.

The female was a little more than 30 years old, which is very old for a giraffe. Mostly, in the wild, they live to be about 15 or 20 years old.

The two young giraffes were born at the zoo. They never knew and will probably never know any other kind of life.

The two older ones and the two mother giraffes had not been born in the zoo, but had been caught in Africa and brought to the zoo. They will probably live longer in the zoo than they would in the wild. There is no danger here, and they are fed and taken care of.

But they will never live a regular giraffe life again, as it is in the wild—wandering from place to place with other giraffes, eating leaves from the tall trees, watching for danger, running with their strong legs swiftly over the flat plains, using their great giraffe bodies as they were meant to be used. Of course, when they became older and slower, they would be brought down, finally, by a lion. But they would have lived a giraffe life as it was meant to be, until the moment they died.

I wonder if the older giraffes ever think back, and remember the life they used to have, and wonder if it will ever be that way again.

You could say that the giraffe is a work of art that has taken nature millions of years to create and to design so that it might survive. Let us hope that they will continue to be one of the many and varied living things that make up the total environment of the Earth.

INDEX

adaptation, 21–25
Africa, 16, 21, 30, 47–48
ancestors of present-day
        giraffe, 19–21
Arabic language, 13
Arabs, 2, 6, 10–11
Artiodactyla (order), 13

behavior, 1, 5
Bengal, King of, 47
birth, 41
Brisson, Mathurin, 11
Bronx Zoo, The, 53–54

calves. *See* young, care and
        development of
"camel-bull-panther," 9
"camelopard," 9, 11
Cervus (genus), 11
Cervus camelopardalis, 11
Charles X, King of France, 1–2
Charleton, Walter, 11
China, 21, 47
classification of animals, 11–17
coat
        color of, 9, 17, 29, 53
        pattern of, 5, 17, 27, 30, 53
comparisons of giraffe to
        other animals, 9–11
Congo pygmies, 16

danger signals, 27, 36
        See also vulnerability
de Beaujeu, Anne (daughter of King
        Louis XI of France), 47
descriptions, historical, 9–11, 47
"double-naming" of animals, 11

eating habits, 33–35, 41
        See also food
Egypt, 1, 9, 47
elephants, 19, 22
enemies, 27, 29, 43, 54
Ethiopic language, 13
"even-toed ungulates," 13–15

evolution of animals, 22–25
extinction of animals, 21–22
eyes, 29

family (scientific classification), 15
Fano zoo, 47
feet, 9–10
        See also hoofs
females, alertness of, 27
fighting
        with enemies, 29, 43
        among males, 43
food, 2, 13, 41, 53
        See also water
fossils, 19, 22
France, 1–6

gait, 5, 27
generic name, 11
gentleness, 1, 5
genus, 15–16
geological changes, effect on animals,
        19
Giraffa camelopardalis, 11
giraffe meat, as food for man, 48
giraffe-shaped god, tribal belief in, 48
Giraffidae family, 15, 19
giraffids, 19–21
        habitat of, 21
        horns of, 21
        necks of, 21
        sizes of, 21
Greece, 9, 21
groups, for traveling, 41

habitat, 16, 21, 27, 29
hair, 5, 48, 53
head, 9–10, 43
hearing, 29
height, 1, 27, 29
hide, uses for, 48
historical descriptions, 9–11, 47–48
hoofs, 10, 13, 43
        See also feet
horns, 9–10, 15–17
horse, 22

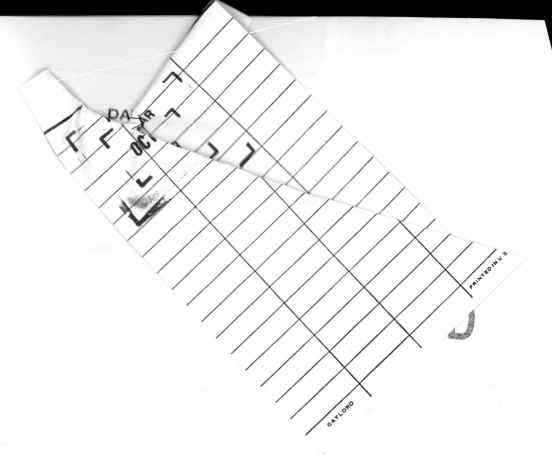